PIRATES ~AND~ TREASURE

Saviour Pirotta

RSVP
RAINTREE
STECK-VAUGHN
PUBLISHERS
The Steck-Vaughn Company

Austin, Texas

THE REMARKABLE WORLD

Dangerous Waters

MONSTERS OF THE DEEP
PIRATES AND TREASURE
VOYAGES OF EXPLORATION
THE WHALERS

U.S. copyright © 1995 Thomson Learning

U.K. copyright © 1995 Wayland (Publishers) Ltd.

This edition published by Raintree Steck-Vaughn Publishers, an imprint of Steck-Vaughn Company

Library of Congress Cataloging-in-Publication Data
Pirotta, Saviour.
Pirates and treasure / Saviour Pirotta.
    p.   cm.—(Remarkable world of—)
Includes bibliographical references and index.
ISBN 0-8172-4820-X
1. Pirates—Juvenile literature. 2. Treasure trove—Juvenile literature. [1. Pirates.] I. Title. II. Series.
G535.P65   1995
910.4'5—dc20   94-48746

Printed in Italy. Bound in the United States.

Picture acknowledgments
AKG, Berlin 4 (bottom); Bridgeman Art Library, London 24 (bottom)/Private Collection, 44 (bottom)/ National Maritime Museum, London; C M Dixon 17 (bottom), 18 (right); Mary Evans Picture Library 18 (left), 36, 45; Eye Ubiquitous 26 (bottom)/P. B. Adams, 44 (top)/John Dakers; Michael Holford 9 (bottom); Ann Ronan at Image Select 8 (center); National Maritime Museum, London *title page*, 11 (bottom), 14, 15, 33 (top), 34 (bottom), 38-9, 40, 42 (bottom); Peter Newark's Historical Pictures 4 (top), 7, 11 (top), 16 (bottom), 19, (bottom), 23 (bottom), 24 (top), 25 (bottom), 26 (top), 27, 28, 30, 31 (top), 31 (bottom), 33 (bottom), 34 (top), 34-5, 37 (bottom), 40-41, 41, 46 (top left), 46 (bottom right); Ronald Sheridan's Photo Library/Ancient Art and Architecture Collection 6, 8 (left), 13, 16 (top), 22 (center), 23 (top), 25 (top), 42 (top); Wayland Picture Library 9 (top), 20 (top), 20 (bottom), 21 (top), 46 (bottom left).

The maps, flags, and other artwork on pages 4, 5, 9, 10, 12, 17, 18 (top), 19 (top), 21 (bottom), 22, 29 (top and bottom), 32, 37 (top), 38, 39 (bottom), 43 and 46 (top center and top right) are by Barbara Loftus.

CONTENTS

PIRATES!

Pirates were so cruel, desperate, and bloodthirsty that they would cut off a man's fingers to steal his gold rings. They were such cunning thieves that they would force a sailor to vomit to see if he had swallowed any small treasures to hide them. Meeting a band of pirates was dangerous and often deadly.

When sailing ships were the only way to go across the ocean, pirates were a terrifying menace.

Ahoy! A gang of wily pirates pose as merchants and their passengers to fool a U.S. Navy ship.

They were men and women who lived by attacking any ship they thought they could take. They would seize anything of value on board—and sometimes even the ship itself. Wherever there were ships and sailors, there were pirates lurking just over the horizon, hungry for treasure and ready to do anything to get it.

The pirates of centuries past have become today's swashbuckling legends, but they were regarded very differently at the time.

In 1837, American Charles Ellms wrote, "In the mind of the mariner, there is a superstitious horror connected with the name of Pirate; and there are few subjects that interest and excite the curiosity of mankind more than the desperate exploits, foul doings, and diabolical careers of these monsters in human form…"

Many pirates started out as ordinary sailors. But with just a few attacks on the right ships they could steal more money than they ever could possibly have earned honestly. Pirates were almost always excellent seafarers. Their ships were often much smaller and carried fewer men than those they attacked. They relied heavily on their sailing skills and careful planning to surprise their victims.

This map shows the main haunts of the pirates, privateers, buccaneers, and corsairs. Many pirates had only one ship. Others traveled in organized fleets to terrorize and rob sailors and traders.

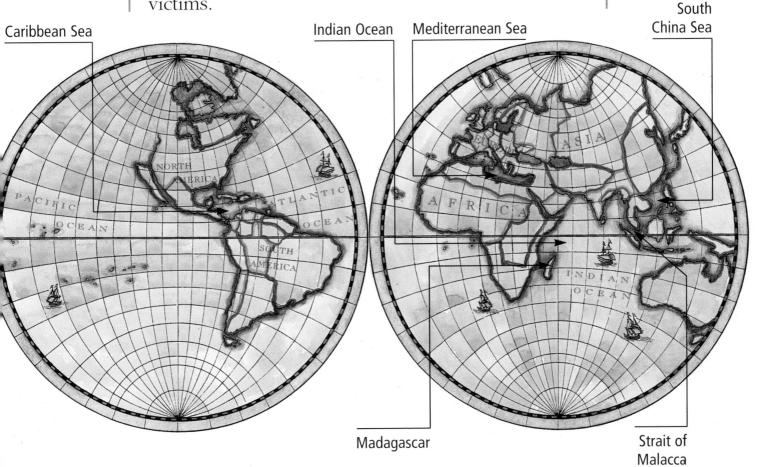

Caribbean Sea

Indian Ocean

Mediterranean Sea

South China Sea

Madagascar

Strait of Malacca

5

Some countries even used pirates to attack ships owned by another country. These pirates were given a permit, or "letter of marque," and could call themselves "privateers"—as if they were waging a private war!

The first pirates

Some of the world's earliest sailors were pirates. Phoenician sailors traveled throughout the Mediterranean from as early as 2000 B.C. They were brave and skillful sea merchants, but they also attacked ships and coastal towns. The ancient Greek poem by Homer, the *Odyssey*, tells of Phoenician pirates kidnapping people from the island of Syra and selling them as slaves.

This carved stone shows a Phoenician trading ship of the first or second century B.C. The Phoenicians used their mighty ships for piracy as well as honest trade. They, in turn, were pounced on by Greek pirates.

The menace of the Mediterranean

Around 150 B.C., a powerful group of rugged pirates emerged along the southeastern coast of Turkey, a region then called Cilicia. By 70 B.C., they had become a menace to trade all over the Mediterranean. They stole Egyptian grain before it reached Rome, where it was badly needed.

6

Caesar's ransom

Around 75 B.C., long before he became dictator of the Roman Empire, Julius Caesar decided to take a vacation on the island of Rhodes, near Greece. On the way, his ship was attacked by pirates. One of them recognized Caesar and the pirates decided to keep Caesar alive and hold him for ransom. Caesar asked how much ransom they would demand. When they told him 20 talents of gold (about $30,000) Caesar was shocked because he didn't think it was enough. Caesar thought a man of his greatness was worth a huge ransom. He told them to demand at least 50 talents.

The pirates did as Caesar suggested. They sent some of his servants to ask for the ransom and locked him up belowdecks with his doctor and two servants. It took Caesar's servants forty days to return with the ransom. By this time the young Roman was tired of sitting in a smelly cabin.

The pirates kept their part of the deal and released Caesar. But as they did Caesar told them that he would hunt them down and crucify each pirate. The pirates laughed at young Caesar's words. Shortly after his release, Caesar gathered some soldiers and hunted the pirates down. When he caught them, he cut their throats and had them all nailed to trees just as he had promised. Then he took his vacation in Rhodes.

In this picture, Roman captives are forced to walk the plank, a famous pirate method of killing captives. In fact, there is little evidence to suggest that real pirates ever used the plank, either in Julius Caesar's time or later.

The Cilician pirates built harbors and fortifications where they could hide their ships and weapons. They grew richer and more bold. In his work *Parallel Lives*, the Greek writer Plutarch described the pirates' vessels: "The ships' masts were covered in gold, their oars gilded with silver, and their sails made of expensive purple cloth..."

The Roman general Pompey's victory over the Cilician pirates made him a hero. This coin bearing his head dates from 49 B.C., a year after his death.

Rowdy Cilician pirates celebrate a successful raid. These greedy bandits attacked towns as well as ships.

By 67 B.C., the Cilician pirates had captured about 400 cities. The Roman senate ordered Pompey, a brilliant Roman general, to get rid of the pirates. Pompey attacked the pirates with vigor. In less than three months most of them had surrendered. Pompey gave those that surrendered some land where they could start a new life as farmers.

THE CORSAIRS

The Battle of Lepanto (below) was the last great battle between Christian and Muslim galleys. It took place on October 7, 1571 in the eastern Mediterranean. Almost 300 Muslim ships were destroyed and 30,000 fighters were killed or captured. The Christian victory was celebrated all over Europe.

A FTER the western part of the Roman Empire fell in the year 476, pirates still haunted the Mediterranean Sea. But their attacks were few and far between compared to those of the Cilician pirates who came before them.

The spread of Islam

In the first half of the seventh century, the Arab prophet Muhammad founded a religion called Islam. The new faith spread quickly throughout the Arab countries and, by the ninth century, it had taken hold in the Middle East and all of North Africa.

This caused fear throughout Europe. Many Christians could not accept the fact that the Holy Land where Jesus Christ had lived was now in Muslim hands. Worse, they were terrified that their own faith and way of life would be swept aside by Islam.

Eastward Ho! Many European noblemen used the holy wars against the Muslims to line their own pockets. Wealthy knights often paid for raiding expeditions to North Africa and then kept a large part of the treasure, or booty, for themselves.

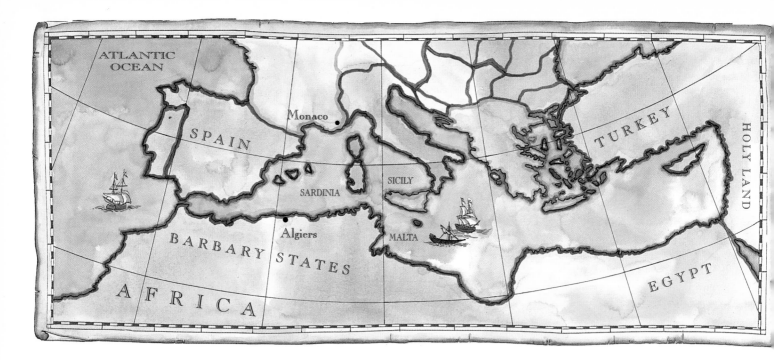

By the early sixteenth century, Muslim pirates had formed a professional brotherhood that caused mayhem along the Mediterranean trade routes. Two hundred years later, the island of Malta (in the center of the map) had become the base for much secret pirate activity organized by the Christian powers.

Centuries of bloodshed followed, as Christians and Muslims fought for control of the countries and trade routes of the Mediterranean. Those years of fighting produced a new kind of pirate—the corsair.

Christian corsairs were employed by Christian governments to attack Muslim ships and cities. In the same way, Muslim governments used their corsairs to plunder Christian ships and cities. Both Christian and Muslim governments considered piracy an effective way of reducing the enemy's power and strengthening their own.

The Muslim corsairs gave a big share of their treasure and profits to the deys, the military leaders of the Muslim Arab countries of North Africa. The Christian corsairs got permission to attack Muslim ships from the governments of Sicily, Monaco, Sardinia, and Spain. Many of them worked for the Knights of Saint John (or the Hospitalers), a military order set up to defend the Christian faith. The knights were paid hefty fees by their corsairs.

Human treasure

The corsairs' favorite booty was human cargo. Slaves were always in demand to work as rowers in the galleys—long, low warships—of Christian and Muslim corsairs. They fetched a good price in the slave markets. If important people were captured they were held for ransom.

Men condemned to the galleys did not live long. Often they were made to row day and night with nothing but bread and water inside them. Those who refused to row were executed immediately. Most people captured by Muslim corsairs were taken to the slave markets on the Barbary Coast. To make sure they did not escape, a heavy ball and chain was lashed to their right legs. Slaves who were not bought by private owners became the property of the state and they had to live in a special place called the bagnio. They were forced to do hard physical work —such as quarrying stone—and were given very little food.

Below: Christian slaves pray to God to help them escape. Prisoners who could not afford to pay for their release sometimes tried to escape in small boats. Lack of fresh water killed many of them. Others were recaptured by passing Muslim ships.

Above: A Muslim pirate forces Christian slaves to row faster. Some people escaped this unbearable torture by paying their Muslim owners huge ransoms. In many countries, organizations were set up to help families raise ransom money to free Christian slaves.

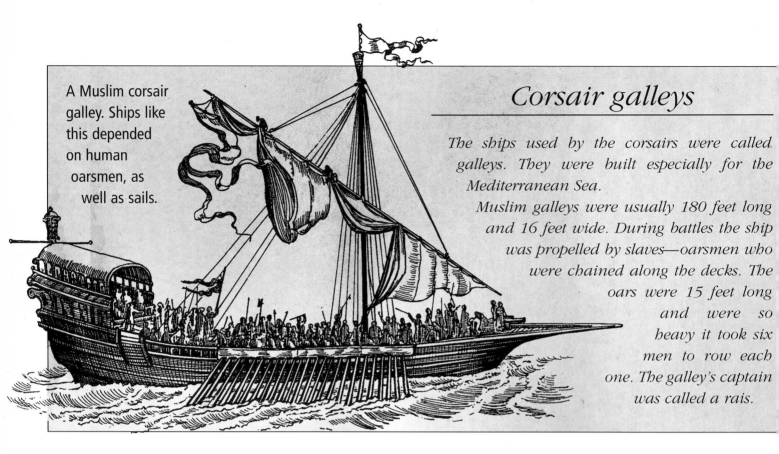

A Muslim corsair galley. Ships like this depended on human oarsmen, as well as sails.

Corsair galleys

The ships used by the corsairs were called galleys. They were built especially for the Mediterranean Sea.

Muslim galleys were usually 180 feet long and 16 feet wide. During battles the ship was propelled by slaves—oarsmen who were chained along the decks. The oars were 15 feet long and were so heavy it took six men to row each one. The galley's captain was called a rais.

Slaves might try to get out of the bagnio by becoming Muslims. But this was a dangerous step to take. If a slave who had "turned Turk" was captured by Christian pirates, he was tortured and killed for joining the enemy.

Muslims captured by Christian corsairs did not fare too well either. Anyone taken by the Knights of Saint John was shipped to Malta, which had the biggest slave market in Europe.

During the seventeenth century many European pirates joined the Muslim corsairs so they could get more booty. These renegades taught the Arabs many of their navigational secrets. One, a Flemish renegade named Simon Danser, showed the Muslim corsairs how to build the powerful "round"

This handsome galley belonged to the Pope. It was heavily armed with cannons.

A Muslim galley had a single cannon on the bow behind a large battering ram. The corsairs usually rammed into the enemy ship and climbed aboard with their muskets and curved swords, called scimitars. They were very good at swordplay and they relied on speed and the element of surprise to win their battles.

Christian galleys were similar to those of the Muslims, but they often had two or three masts instead of the Muslim galleys' one. They had more cannons, too, since the Christian corsairs preferred gunfighting to hand-to-hand combat. The Maltese pirates were especially renowned for their gunnery skills. The hulls of all galleys needed scraping and waxing frequently to help them cut through water easily.

ships used in Northern Europe. With these, the corsairs were able to break out into the Atlantic Ocean and attack countries like England, Ireland, and Iceland. Another renegade, John Ward, was an ex-privateer. He joined the corsairs of the dey of Tunis because he missed his privateering days "...when the whole sea was our Empire, where we robb'd at will..." and could "...sing, swear, drink...and kill men as freely as your cakemakers do flies."

The bold, bad Barbarossa brothers

In the first half of the sixteenth century, Aruj and Khair-ed-din Barbarossa were the most famous—and the most feared—corsairs in the Mediterranean.

The Barbarossa brothers were the most feared Muslim pirates in the world. Aruj (left) was captured by the Knights of Saint John. He was ransomed and became a ruthless captain. His younger brother, Khair-ed-din (right), succeeded him.

In 1504, Aruj enraged the Western world when he captured two treasure ships belonging to the head of the Catholic Church—Pope Julius II. This success led to many more.

After a number of years, the Barbarossa brothers were asked to go to the aid of the Dey of Algiers. The Spanish, tired of losing ships to the Muslims, had landed soldiers and built a fort overlooking Algiers. The Algerian corsairs could no longer sail in and out of their harbor.

Aruj attacked the fort, but the Spanish pushed his soldiers back. Then the unruly pirates started to fight among themselves and also attacked Algerians. The dey of Algiers decided it was better to have the Spanish occupying his harbor than the horrible pirates. He asked the Spanish to help him destroy the Barbarossa brothers. But the pirates discovered the plot and seized the city. Then they destroyed the Spanish forces sent to fight them. The Barbarossas grew so bold that they attacked any ship they saw, and the treasure chests of Barbary overflowed with their loot.

Finally the Spanish sent a fleet of galleons and 10,000 soldiers to get rid of the Barbarossas once and for all. The Spanish galleons were built to sail on the Atlantic Ocean and were much stronger than Aruj's ships. As the galleons approached Algiers, Aruj ordered his men to pick up their treasure and flee. It was a big mistake. The Spanish soldiers, with nothing to weigh them down, caught up with the pirates as they were crossing a river. The corsairs who hadn't crossed were trapped, and all of them, including Aruj, were killed.

Khair-ed-din had escaped to the other side of the river, and he vowed to avenge his brother's death. People said he became a better leader than his brother. The Spanish had no choice but to come back and try to destroy him as well. But the pirates had stolen guns and ammunition from Spanish ships and they used the Spaniards' own weapons to defeat them. When the Sultan of Turkey asked Khair-ed-din to take charge of his fleet and make it the finest in the Mediterranean, Barbarossa accepted. It is said that he lived in comfort well into old age.

A Spanish galleon battles with a Muslim ship. The Spaniards, who regularly sailed to their bases in Italy, were frequent targets of the corsairs.

Dragut's deadly grapes

Dragut Rais

Dragut Rais was a lieutenant of Khair-ed-din Barbarossa. He had been a slave of one of the Christian corsairs, but had become a brilliant and ruthless corsair himself. From 1547 to 1565, he led numerous attacks on Christian ports and harbors, mostly on the island of Malta.

Dragut was very fierce. A legend from the Maltese island of Gozo says that one day he spied a grape vine on the island as he was sailing nearby on his galley. Dragut decided he wanted the grapes for his supper. He ordered a young pirate to swim ashore and get them.

The pirate did as he was told. But in the process of picking the grapes he broke the vine's stem. For some reason, Dragut was utterly furious. He ordered his crew to take the brave pirate back to the vineyard and have him burned alive.

The end of the corsairs

During the eighteenth century the French and British governments began sending ships to the Mediterranean. As more countries fell under European influence and control, the corsairs found themselves beset by these navies. One by one, the Arab countries gave up piracy and slavery, and the Christian corsairs disappeared too. The last corsairs were rounded up in 1830, when Algiers was invaded by French forces.

Left: Stephen Decatur of the U.S. Navy attacks a corsair frigate near Tripoli, North Africa, in 1804. The Americans resented losing their trading ships to the Muslim corsairs or paying bribes for safe passage. They swore to destroy the pirates.

THE SPANISH MAIN

IN the summer of 1523, French pirate Jean Florin ordered his crew to attack three Spanish ships off Cape Saint Vincent in southwest Portugal. The pirates' haul included three chests full of gold ingots, 500 pounds of gold dust, 680 pounds of pearls, emeralds, weapons, expensive cloth, and animals. This booty had been taken from the Aztecs by the Spanish.

The Spanish did not allow other Europeans to trade with their colonies. Settlers on their land were attacked and killed.

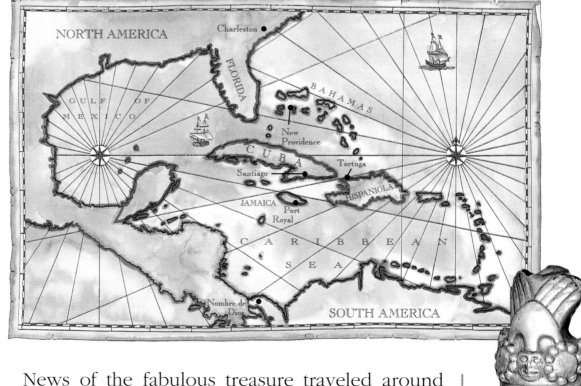

Right: The Spanish Main

Below: Spanish soldiers load their mighty galleons with treasure chests bound for the city of Seville in Spain. Emeralds and pearls were often transported in simple sacks.

News of the fabulous treasure traveled around the world. The Spanish were furious. Since Christopher Columbus had sailed to the Americas in 1492, Spain had laid claim to what it called the Spanish Main—the American mainland, the West Indies, the Gulf of Mexico, and the Caribbean with all its islands. Spaniards had established settlements with farms, silver mines, and plantations and had stolen treasures from the native Americans. The fabulous riches plundered from the Spanish Main were sent back to Spain in large galleons.

Cheaters and thieves

The men who went to ransack Spanish treasure ships were not called pirates, except by the Spaniards. They were privateers, who gave most of the booty they captured to their masters—usually governments

Above: When the Spanish brought treasures like this silver statue to Europe, rumors of a "river of silver and gold" pouring into Spain whipped the Western world into a jealous frenzy.

hostile to Spain—and kept only a small part for themselves. Even so, privateers could become very rich. They often cheated and stole treasure without official permission. But their masters probably overlooked such thievery since the privateers brought in so much money.

The Spanish threatened to hang anyone who robbed their ships, but this did not stop the English and French privateers. So, from 1543, the Spanish ships traveled in large fleets to frighten the pirates.

Above: A Spanish galleon. These large ships helped to make Spain the ruler of the oceans for centuries.

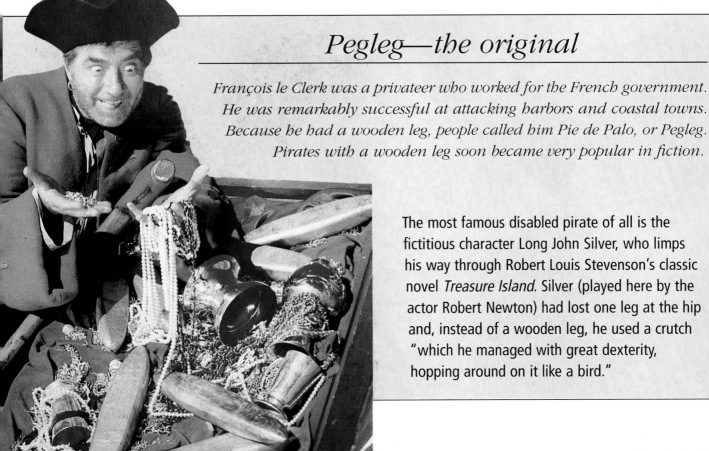

Pegleg—the original

François le Clerk was a privateer who worked for the French government. He was remarkably successful at attacking harbors and coastal towns. Because he had a wooden leg, people called him Pie de Palo, or Pegleg. Pirates with a wooden leg soon became very popular in fiction.

The most famous disabled pirate of all is the fictitious character Long John Silver, who limps his way through Robert Louis Stevenson's classic novel *Treasure Island.* Silver (played here by the actor Robert Newton) had lost one leg at the hip and, instead of a wooden leg, he used a crutch "which he managed with great dexterity, hopping around on it like a bird."

This made attacks at sea much more difficult for the privateers, and they started attacking the ports of the Spanish Main instead.

"My Dear Pirate"

Francis Drake began his seafaring career accompanying his cousin John Hawkins, who sold African slaves to Spanish plantations in the Caribbean. When Drake went out on his own expedition in 1570 he attacked Spanish treasure ships. After one expedition Drake brought back a huge haul of treasure—of which the English Queen, Elizabeth I, received £300,000 and he kept £10,000.

Now Drake wanted to capture the city of Nombre de Dios (in the north of modern Panama), where the Spanish kept most of the treasure awaiting transport to Spain. His first attempt did not go according to plan: as he attacked the city he was shot in the leg and had to turn back. Then Drake heard that a mule train carried Spanish gold from the mines in Panama to Nombre de Dios. He and his men prepared to ambush the mule train. Just as the mules were approaching, one of his men fell out of the bushes and cursed loudly. The Spanish heard him and

Right: The constant looting of Spanish ships by English sailors, especially Drake, provoked King Philip II of Spain into sending an Armada of 130 ships to invade England. It was a dismal failure, with half the fleet lost.

the mule train got away safely. With the help of a French privateer, Guillaume de Testu, Drake attacked the mule train again as it reached Nombre de Dios. This time he captured the gold.

Drake went on to attack many more mule trains and Spanish treasure ships. Queen Elizabeth made him a knight. She even gave him a special sword to use on her enemies. In private, she referred to him as "my dear pirate."

A pirate's rules of conduct

Before joining a ship, many pirates had to swear to obey the ship's code of conduct. It forced them to live by rules very similar to those set out in privateers' contracts.

In a book entitled A General History of the Robberies and Murders of the Most Notorious Pirates, *published in 1724, Captain Charles Johnson described the pirates' code of conduct. Here is a summary of some of the rules:*

- The Captain shall have one full share and a half in all prizes; the master, carpenter, boatswain, and gunner shall have one share and a quarter.
- Men caught stealing from the ship's coffers will have their noses slit and will be marooned on a desert island.
- If anyone tries to run away he will be marooned on an island with one bottle of powder, one flask of water, and one small firearm. Anyone caught attempting to desert ship during a battle will be executed.

- No one is allowed to leave until the ship has £1,000 worth of booty.
- Lights and candles are to be extinguished by 8 o'clock every night. Anyone who wants to go on drinking must do it on deck by moonlight.
- Any musicians hired to entertain the crew are to have Sunday off. The rest of the week they must play every night.
- Any fool trying to smuggle his wife aboard disguised as a man will be put to death immediately.

THE BUCCANEERS

IN 1630 Spain signed a treaty allowing England and France to colonize some of the lands in what had been the Spanish Main. But the fighting and the looting among the nations continued. The arrival of African slaves and cheap labor in the Spanish Main left a lot of European settlers without jobs. They drifted to the Caribbean island of Hispaniola (now Haiti and the Dominican Republic), where many runaway slaves, deserters, and criminals lived.

On Hispaniola, the pigs introduced by the Spanish had multiplied in great numbers, providing food for everyone. The Arawak Indians taught the men how to barbecue the pigs on an open fire called a *buccan* or *boucan*. This soon became their favorite dish and people began to call the settlers buccaneers.

Some of the buccaneers started to sell dried and smoked pork to passing privateer ships. The Spanish did not want their enemies to be able to restock this way, so during the 1630s they attacked Hispaniola and destroyed the pigs. The buccaneers fled to the small island of Tortuga off the northeast coast of Hispaniola. One of them, called Pierre le Grand, attacked a Spanish galleon and made off with its

A buccaneer on the island of Hispaniola. His musket and dogs were used for hunting cattle and pigs, which were then barbecued (see the small inset picture).

22

treasure. He had crept up on the galleon in a small sailboat called a pinnace. The galleon's crew was caught by surprise and Pierre took the ship with just a handful of men. With enough loot to last him the rest of his life, Pierre sailed back home to France.

A buccaneer keeps a lookout for ships passing the island of Tortuga.

The Brethren of the Coast

Soon the other buccaneers took to piracy, calling themselves the Brethren of the Coast. Tortuga became their headquarters. The buccaneers wanted to try a new way of life—one that was fair to everyone. So all the doors and treasure chests on Tortuga were kept open. Before every raid, all the pirates met to discuss the plan of attack. Their leader, who was called the Admiral of the Black, listened to everyone's suggestions.

"One for you, one for me." The pirates dole out the booty after a raid. Some retired to live in splendor on their ill-gotten gains. But many wasted their share of the treasure the moment they laid their hands on it.

The buccaneers often crept up on unsuspecting galleons in small boats called pinnaces, to take Spanish crews by surprise. Sometimes they succeeded in taking over a ship before most of the crew even realized they were under attack.

Many buccaneers had free insurance against accident and bodily harm. A man who lost his right hand was given 600 pieces of eight (valuable silver coins) in compensation. If he lost his left arm, he got 500 pieces of eight. These were vast sums of money in the seventeenth century.

As the buccaneers grew bolder and greater in number, they moved to the island of Jamaica, which had been captured from the Spanish by the British. The British officers welcomed the buccaneers. They knew the Spanish would not dare attack Jamaica if their harbor was filled with pirate ships.

Jamaica was a good home for the buccaneers, most of whom were English. Its main harbor, Port Royal, was ideally placed for attacking Spanish ships, and the governors of the island gave the buccaneers written permission to loot enemy ships.

Fabulous loot

The fabulous hauls stolen from the Spanish tresure ships included silver, gold, pearls,

Pirates swarming aboard a Spanish galleon. They were mainly after gold and silver, but they would also steal other useful things like sails, ropes, medicine, food, and even furniture.

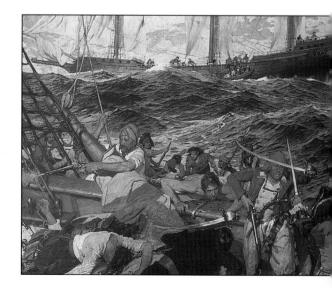

emeralds, and pieces of eight. The English privateer Sir Christopher Mings was given permission by the Governor of Jamaica to attack Spanish targets on England's behalf. After one raid on Santiago in Cuba, he returned home with seven chests full of silver.

Merchant ships carried other cargo, including expensive linen and velvet, wine, brandy, and all kinds of preserved food, which could be almost as valuable as treasure. In 1630, Captain John Smith described the capture of a Venetian ship by pirates: "The silks, velvets, cloth of gold and tissue, piastres, sequins, and sultanies, which is gold and silver, that they unloaded in four-and-twenty hours was wonderful…"

The end of buccaneering in the Caribbean

In the last years of the seventeenth century, the Spanish lost much of their power and land in and

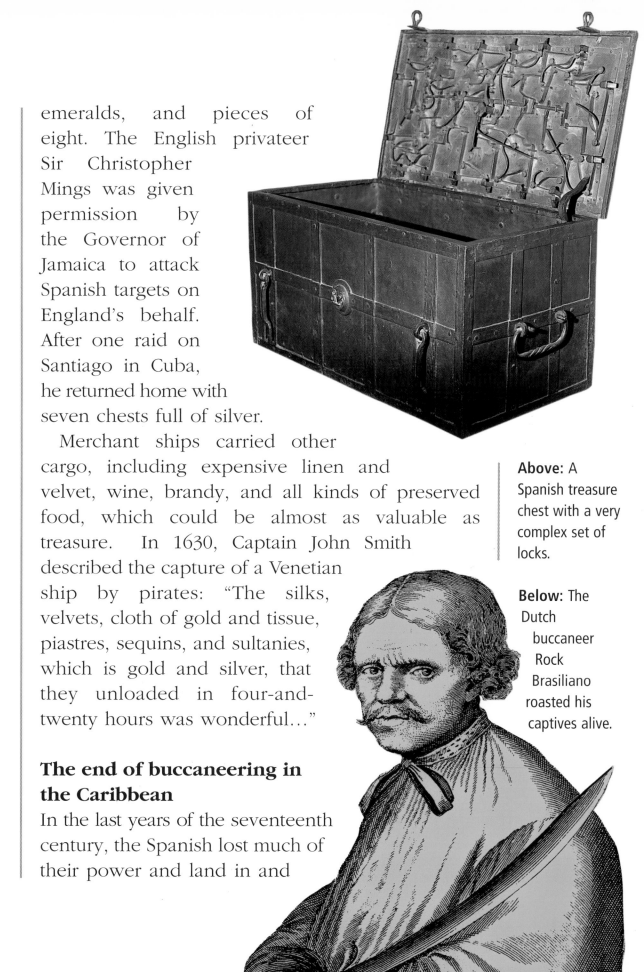

Above: A Spanish treasure chest with a very complex set of locks.

Below: The Dutch buccaneer Rock Brasiliano roasted his captives alive.

Henry Morgan (c.1635-1688)

Henry Morgan was born in Wales and ran away to sea when still a young boy. In his teens, he joined a pirate ship bound for the island of Tortuga. There Morgan swore the secret oath and became one of the Brethren of the Coast.

Morgan and his new friends soon had enough money to deck out their own ship with guns and provisions. He was made captain of the first raid. This was a success, and many more were to follow. Morgan was then made vice admiral of the buccaneer fleet. He became incredibly rich, bought a plantation in Jamaica, and owned many slaves. He dressed like a gentleman and rubbed marigold paste in his hair as a kind of perfume.

In 1668, Sir Thomas Modyford, the Governor of Jamaica, offered Morgan a letter of marque—a document stating that Morgan was now a privateer acting on behalf of England. Modyford had heard that the Spanish were about to attack Jamaica. He wanted Morgan to attack the Spanish first and share the booty with him.

With just 300 men, Morgan overcame the Spanish city of Portobello in Panama and returned to Jamaica with a huge haul of treasure, including 300 slaves. Sir Thomas Modyford was very pleased. Morgan then raided the city of Maracaibo on the Venezuelan coast. But the way out was blocked by several ships, three of which had been sent by the governor of Panama himself. Morgan had his men clean out a captured merchant ship and fill its hold with pitch, tar, and sulphur. The decks were crammed with kegs of gunpowder. Fake cannons were made out of Indian drums and placed in the portholes. The men made dummy pirates with pumpkins for heads—a dummy of Morgan was put on the quarterdeck.

around the Caribbean Sea. There were fewer ships to attack, and they no longer had holds packed with treasure. Privateering gradually came to an end as countries relied more on full-time navies. Many buccaneers were lured away to the Indian Ocean by rumors of new treasures. A few stayed on, but the buccaneers' profitable days of plundering Spanish treasure galleons were over.

Soon the ship looked ready for action. A handful of brave men steered it toward the Spanish galleons. Just before coming alongside, the men lit fuses attached to barrels of gunpowder and made off in small boats. The Spaniards fired. Suddenly there was a terrible explosion. The ship blew up, destroying first one, then another Spanish galleon. The battle that followed raged for days, but Morgan and his men managed to escape.

When the buccaneer announced he was going to attack Panama itself, 2,200 men volunteered to join his crew. Morgan's fleet set sail in December 1670. The raid was a total success, and afterward Morgan settled down on his plantation, only setting sail now to attack his former buccaneer friends. King Charles II was so impressed by Morgan that he knighted him. Sir Henry Morgan returned to Jamaica as Deputy Governor and died a contented man in 1688.

Henry Morgan's buccaneers ransack the burning town of Panama in 1670. Their massive haul included silk, diamonds, and hundreds of prisoners.

Left: The buccaneer captain Blackbeard's castle on St. Thomas in the Virgin Islands is now open to visitors.

A mean, mad dog

Piracy flourished once more in the Caribbean after the Treaty of Utrecht, which was signed in 1713. This treaty ended the War of the Spanish Succession between Spain, France, and Britain. When the fighting was over, many sailors found themselves out of work and penniless. Some of them chose to earn their living by taking up piracy.

Before he went into battle, Blackbeard used to stick lighted tapers in his hair. They belched out black smoke as they burned, scaring his enemies out of their wits. He also wore six pistols strapped across his chest.

One particularly fierce group of pirates set up a colony on New Providence, an island in the Bahamas. They attacked any ship they encountered, whatever its nationality. One of these pirates was called Blackbeard.

Blackbeard's real name was Edward Teach. He was born in England around 1680 and began his career as a privateer. After the Treaty of Utrecht, he joined the crew of a pirate ship. The captain, Benjamin Hornigold, was impressed by Blackbeard, who didn't waste time waiting for victims to take their rings off—he just chopped off their fingers and dropped them in his pocket. When the pirates captured a sloop, Blackbeard was made its captain.

The two ships looted in the Caribbean until they captured a large French ship that Blackbeard made his own, renaming it *Queen Anne's Revenge*. After the battle, Hornigold gave up piracy, but Blackbeard carried on. In May 1718 he blockaded the harbor of Charleston, South Carolina, taking hostages. The townspeople had to pay a ransom.

Blackbeard and his men had so much treasure that they wanted to go ashore and enjoy some of it. They sailed up the Pamlico River to the town of Bath in North Carolina and asked King George I for

A group of buccaneers aboard their ship. Pirate ships were often merchant vessels that had been captured during previous attacks.

Pirates liked fast ships and especially vessels with a shallow draught so that they could be hidden in bays and small inlets.

a royal pardon (North Carolina was then a British colony). It was granted, but Blackbeard still sailed up and down the Pamlico River, stealing from plantations on the way. In despair, the local people sent for help to the neighboring colony of Virginia.

The Jolly Roger

The pirates' famous black flag probably takes its name from the French Joli Rouge (or "pretty red"), which was a blood-red flag flown by pirates who intended to kill everyone on board a ship they were about to attack. There were actually many different Jolly Roger flags. Blackbeard's flag showed a skeleton with an hourglass in one hand and, in the other, a dart piercing a heart with three drops of blood dripping from it.

The pirate Bartholomew Roberts was furious with the governors of Barbados and Martinique because of their constant attempts to capture him. He had a new flag made for his ship, "with his own figure portrayed standing upon two skulls, and under them the letters ABH and AMH, signifying A Barbadian's Head and A Martinican's Head."

Pirates often had their own versions of the Jolly Roger, but all were guaranteed to strike terror into sailors' hearts. These are the flags of Christopher Condent (top row), Blackbeard and Thomas Tew (second row), and "Calico Jack" Rackham and Stede Bonnet (third row). The bottom flag belonged to the Muslim corsairs.

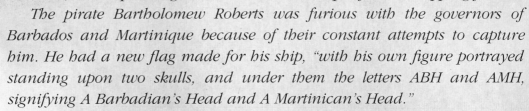

The governor there contacted a British Navy officer, Captain Gordon, whose ship HMS *Pearl* was in the area. Gordon chose his most experienced officer, Lieutenant Robert Maynard, to lead an expedition against Blackbeard.

Maynard tracked the pirate to his hideout in a bay called Ocracoke Inlet in Pamlico Sound. A bloody battle followed. Maynard's men eventually got the upper hand, although Blackbeard fought like a mad dog. He received 20 cutlass wounds and five pistol shots before he died. The next day Blackbeard's head was hung from the bow of

Right
Blackbeard meets his violent end. No one knows where the infamous pirate hid his vast treasure. He used to boast to his friends that only he and the devil knew where it was.

Mary Read

Women pirates

Mary Read and Anne Bonny both sailed the seas dressed as men. Read was born at Plymouth around 1690. Even as a child, she never wore dresses or petticoats—her mother made her dress up as a boy, in order to claim an inheritance for which only a boy was eligible. Read ran away and—pretending to be a man—eventually joined the crew of a Flemish ship going to the West Indies.

Halfway across the ocean, the ship was attacked by British pirates. Read threw away her Flemish cap and joined them. She worked as a pirate until 1717, when King George I of England issued a pardon to all pirates if they left the sea. Mary retired to live in the West Indies, but she ran out of money and went back to piracy. One day she joined the ship of the infamous buccaneer John Rackham. He was nicknamed Calico Jack because he wore brightly

Maynard's ship. The 15 pirates who survived were tried, and most were put to death, although accounts vary as to how many were hanged.

In the years that followed, the British Navy continued to hunt down the pirates of the Caribbean and North America. Many were hanged or put in prison; a few were pardoned. From then on, the Indian Ocean and the China Sea became the main haunts of pirates.

colored clothes made of calico. To her surprise, Read found there was another woman pirate on the ship—Anne Bonny.

Bonny told Read she had been born in County Cork, Ireland. Her father had emigrated to South Carolina—he was a wealthy and respected man. But when Bonny grew up, she fell in love with a sailor and ran away with him to New Providence in the Bahamas, where they got married. Bonny's marriage did not last long. The island was full of pirates and she fell in love with Calico Jack and his treasure.

Read and Bonny became firm friends. With Calico Jack they looted together until, in 1720, their ship was captured by a British Navy vessel and towed to Jamaica. The crew, along with Read, Bonny, and Calico Jack, were sentenced to hang. But Bonny and Read both revealed they were pregnant, and their sentence was changed to imprisonment. Read died in prison shortly afterward, but nothing more is known of Bonny. She was perhaps the toughest of the three—and said of Jack: "If he had fought like a man, he need not have been hanged like a dog."

Anne Bonny

31

FINDING NEW TERRITORY

The lands around the Indian Ocean have been a hive of pirate activity for thousands of years. Piracy in these dangerous waters continues to this day.

WHEN buccaneers from the Caribbean made their way to the Indian Ocean, they discovered that local robbers had been working the Eastern seas for centuries. Marco Polo, a Venetian traveler, had reported seeing pirates from Gujarat and the Malabar Coast of India as early as 1290:

"Twenty pirate ships will set sail with 5 miles between each of them, thus managing to dominate 100 miles of sea. As soon as one of them sights a cargo ship, the others are alerted by means of rockets and lights, so the cargo ship has no chance of getting past...The Gujarati pirates...force the merchants to drink a mixture of tamarind and sea water until they are violently sick. The pirates examine the vomit to see if they can find any pearls or precious stones, as they know that when the merchants are captured they swallow the jewels so as not to be found with them."

Pirates in the Indian Ocean

In 1497, a Portuguese explorer called Vasco da Gama sailed around the Cape of Good Hope and into the Indian Ocean. As a Christian, Vasco da Gama considered himself superior to the local merchants who worshipped gods that were strange to him. He saw no wrong in plundering their ships and stealing their goods. Although da Gama was himself attacked by pirates, a tidal wave of European adventurers followed in his wake. The European "traders" were happy to make money in any way they could—including piracy.

By the 1600s, the situation was so out of control that various kingdoms along the coast were forced to act. By now, the Dutch and the English had taken over from the Portuguese traders. The Dutch had set up the Dutch East India Trading Company to establish permanent trading settlements in the East. The British, not to be outdone, set up the British East India Company. Shah Jahan, the Mogul emperor of India, ordered both companies to clear the sea of pirates or stop trading completely.

The first fleet of the British East India Company left Woolwich, England, in 1601. Its mission was to trade with countries in the East and to rid the Indian Ocean of pirates.

In 1498, the Portuguese explorer Vasco da Gama attacked and looted an Indian ship off the coast of Africa. He then became the target of pirates from Goa in India.

Above: The blunderbuss was the pirates' favorite firearm in the eighteenth century.

Below: Pirates often used swords like these after they had boarded a ship.

While the British East India Company tried to defeat the pirates, King Charles I of England was secretly sending his own privateers to the Indian Ocean. And many British businessmen, jealous of the East India Comany's success, were doing the same. To make matters worse, the Dutch turned a blind eye if they saw pirates looting rival ships.

Many pirates were officially privateers acting on behalf of English governors. They settled on the island of Madagascar, from where they could attack passing ships. Soon they started plundering East India Company ships.

The attacks on these ships had to be planned carefully. An East India Company ship on its way to do business was often laden with gold, silver, and food for the crew. But a ship returning home with new cargo was likely to be packed with useless luxuries such as spices and silks, which were hard to sell.

The notorious Henry Avery

In September 1695, buccaneers captained by Henry Avery attacked two Muslim ships returning to India. The bigger of the two turned out to be the *Gang-i-Sawai*. It carried 600 pilgrims returning from the holy places at Mecca. Despite its size and firepower, the ship did not put up much of a fight; the captain did not want to endanger his passengers.

The *Gang-i-Sawai* belonged to Aurangzeb, the Mogul emperor, and its cargo was worth £325,000. The pirates stole everything, and the emperor was beside himself with rage. He decided to put a stop to trade with England and threw all the British merchants in the city of Surat into prison.

A group of British businessmen in New York came up with a plan. They persuaded Captain William Kidd, a fifty-year-old former privateer, to lead a mission against Avery. At first, Kidd did not like the idea; he had retired from privateering and now owned a very successful shipping business. But the businessmen insisted. Any patriot would try to capture the pirates, they said. And besides, Kidd would be allowed to keep a large share of any booty he took from them.

The notorious pirate Henry Avery was born around 1665. After his attack on the *Gang-i-Sawai* in the Red Sea in 1695, he returned to England with his loot. Although he was never caught, it is thought that merchants swindled him out of his treasure, and he died penniless in Bristol, England, about 1728.

Captain Kidd buries his treasure on Gardiners Island in America. According to legend, it is guarded by the ghost of a dead pirate.

The riddle of Kidd and the pirates

So, in the spring of 1696, William Kidd set out from New York at the helm of the *Adventure Galley*. In his pocket was a list of wanted men. He was determined to bring them all to justice—or was he? Kidd either sailed past Madagascar without trying to capture any pirates or arrived to find no pirates to capture. A little later, however, he attacked and robbed two merchant ships, one of which was called the *Quedah Merchant*. Kidd and his crew made off with £10,000 worth of treasure.

News of this attack soon reached the Mogul emperor, who again threatened to stop trade with England. The British government issued a warrant for Kidd's arrest. Kidd spent some time in Madagascar with Robert Culliford and other pirates before returning to America in 1699. As soon as he arrived, he was arrested and sent to England to stand trial for piracy. He admitted to looting vessels but insisted that it was the crew who had forced him into piracy. He said that he had only attacked the two Arab ships because they were flying French flags. France had been at war with England, and Kidd claimed that he had plundered their cargo as an act of war.

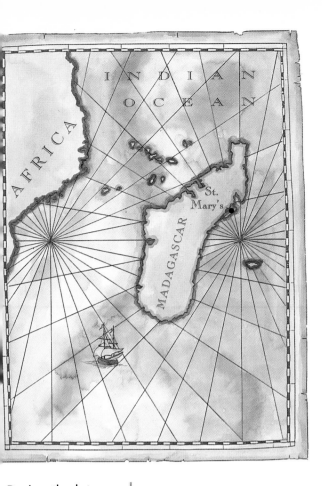

During the late seventeenth and early eighteenth centuries, the island of Madagascar became the main base for pirates who had left the Caribbean. The small island of St. Mary's was where most pirates lived— perhaps as many as 1,500 of them at various times.

No one believed his story. The documents showing that the *Quedah Merchant* was under French protection had been lost. The crew swore that Kidd had forced them to pillage and loot. One man claimed that Kidd had secretly hidden a chest full of gold on Gardiners Island at the tip of Long Island, New York. Others said he had buried many more chests along the banks of the Hudson River.

The jury sided with the sailors. In 1701 Kidd was found guilty and hanged. His body was then dipped in tar to preserve it and was hung in an iron cage at Tilbury, England. It remained there for many years, a grim warning to any would-be pirates of the punishment for their crime.

No one has ever found the mysterious treasure chests that Kidd is supposed to have hidden. And, a few years after his execution, the French documents from the *Quedah Merchant* were found. Was Kidd telling the truth after all?

William Kidd's body suspended from the gallows in Tilbury, England, after his death. When he was hanged at Execution Dock in Wapping, England, hundreds of people went to watch. He had to be hanged twice because the rope snapped in the first attempt and Kidd fell into the mud below.

THE FIERCEST PIRATES OF THE EAST

A Boatload of

For many centuries, the coastal areas of China, and especially the South China Sea, have been home to some of the most ruthless pirates the world has known.

FOR hundreds of years, Chinese and Japanese pirates used to attack each other's ships as well as harbors and coastal towns. The pirates often traveled in huge fleets controlled by powerful warlords. European sailors—explorers, merchants, and pirates—arrived in the region from the fifteenth century onward.

In 1518 a Portuguese pirate named Simon de Andrada built a fort near Macao, in southern China, and began plundering passing ships. He was rooted out three years later, but more European pirates and privateers—especially the Dutch and the British—soon came to take his place. Even some "respectable" sea captains who were acting on behalf of the East India Company would rob ships and keep the profits.

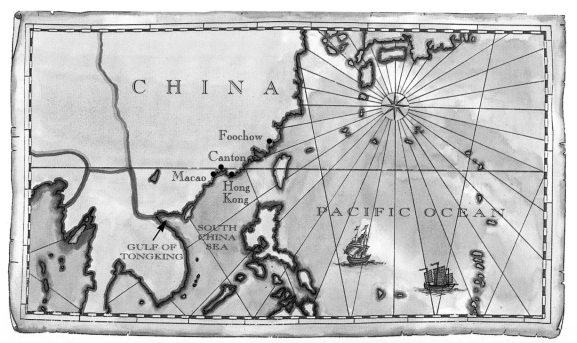

A boatload of Chinese pirates awaits a passing ship. Many poor Chinese turned to piracy as a means of survival.

Chinese pirates

In the seventeenth century, the greatest of the sea robbers in the East was a Chinese pirate, Cheng Chih-lung. He had worked as an interpreter for the East India Company during the 1620s. Cheng's uncle, who owned a small fleet of junks, invited Cheng to go on a pirate voyage with him. Cheng proved to be a fine pirate.

Soon Cheng Chih-lung had a powerful fleet of over 1,000 junks. His men terrorized the coast of China all the way from the Yangtze River to Canton. He lived in luxury, looked after by 300 black servants and protected by an army of Dutch soldiers. Then Cheng got an invitation to work for the Tartars who had just invaded China. Cheng traveled to Foochow to take up his position. But the invitation was a trick. When he arrived, Cheng was seized by the Tartars and then thrown into prison. His fleet of pirate junks was immediately taken over by his son, Cheng Ch'eng-kung

Most Chinese pirates used small, swift junks like this one. They were basically trading junks that had been captured and modified by adding guns.

(known in the West as Koxinga). When Cheng Chih-lung was beheaded in 1661, Koxinga and his pirates created so much havoc that all the local villages along the coast had to be moved 12 miles inland.

When Koxinga died in 1662, his son took over the pirate fleet. But many pirates were not happy under his rule, and they decided to go their own way. Soon the fleet was broken up. No great pirate leader made his mark again until the arrival of Ching Yih in the early years of the nineteenth century.

Unlike the buccaneers, Chinese pirates had colorful flags that often had pictures of their captains. The flag above may have belonged to Shap-'ng-tsai, leader of the last great Chinese pirate fleet.

Ching Yih

Ching Yih, owned 600 junks divided into six smaller fleets, some of which were led by women pirates. Each fleet had its own flag and plundered a different part of the Chinese coast. The main ship in each fleet carried twelve guns and a supply of rowing boats. These boats were armed with swivel guns and could hold up to twenty men for an attack.

Ching Yih and his pirates operated very much like the pirates in other oceans. Sailors who gave in without a fight were allowed to go as soon as their cargo was taken. Those who tried to harm the pirates, however, were often tortured and killed.

John Turner, a British officer who was taken prisoner by Ching Yih's men in 1806, described how he saw the pirates nail a Chinese naval officer's feet to the deck. The pirates beat the man senseless, then took him ashore and cut him to pieces.

Below: A street in Hong Kong in the nineteenth century. The British set up a permanent trading base there in 1841. As trade increased, many pirates were attracted to the area.

The iron rule of Ching Shih

When Ching Yih was killed during a fierce tropical storm, his fleet passed into the hands of Ching Shih, his wife. She proved to be even more bloodthirsty than her husband. She was also a very good administrator, and she kept accurate records of all her looting and bartering.

To keep control of her fleet, Ching Shih drew up a list of orders her pirates had to obey. No one could go ashore without permission, unless they wanted their ears cut off. And no man could abuse a woman; if he wanted one of the prisoners for a wife, he had to buy her.

Ching Shih was so successful that she nearly brought all the trade on the Chinese coast to a complete stop. In the end, her power was destroyed by a bitter feud between two of her pirate captains.

Above: Madame Ching battles it out with a sailor. At the height of her power, Ching Shih is thought to have commanded 800 large junks, almost 1,000 smaller boats, and up to 80,000 pirates, although accounts disagree on how large her fleet was.

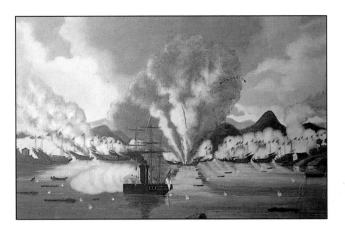

Above: A fleet of Chinese pirate ships goes up in smoke during a battle with the Chinese and British navies in 1849. In the foreground is a heavily armed British paddle wheeler.

With their fleets weakened, Ching Shih and her pirate captains handed over their ships to the Chinese government in 1811. Some of them were pardoned and made naval officers—working to clear the sea of other pirates. It is thought that Ching Shih spent her last years as a smuggler.

Thirty years after Ching Shih's surrender, a new pirate appeared. His name was Shap-'ng-tsai. His fleet attacked many ships and coastal settlements south of Canton. In 1849, the Chinese authorities and the British Navy chased him 1,000 miles before cornering him in the Gulf of Tongking. By that time the British were using paddle wheelers, and Shap-'ng-tsai didn't stand a chance. His fleet of junks was smashed to pieces and 1,800 pirates died. Shap-'ng-tsai, however, managed to escape and found a job with the Chinese government. No other great pirate leader rose to take his place.

Below: A British Navy ship fires broadsides into junks in the pirate fleet of Chui Apoo, the lieutenant of Shap-'ng-tsai, during the great pirate purge of 1849. Although Chui Apoo escaped, his fleet was destroyed and his stockpile of weapons was captured. Shortly afterward, Shap-'ng-tsai himself was defeated.

The islands around Borneo were the home of the Balanini pirates, who used to travel in swift boats called *corocoros*. The Balaninis captured people from the nearby Philippines and sold them as slaves. Their lair on the island of Jolo was destroyed by the Spanish in 1851. For centuries, the Strait of Malacca has been notorious for pirate attacks—and it still is today.

Malaccan pirates

For centuries, the islands of Southeast Asia had traded with one another—and piracy had been part of the trade. Slaves, as well as valuable cargoes, were stolen from the ships of one country and sold to another.

When the Dutch and the English traders came to the islands in the early nineteenth century, they put many local traders out of business. These local traders reacted by turning to piracy.

To reach China and Japan, traders had to pass through the Strait of Malacca between Malaysia and Sumatra. For many years this was considered to be the most dangerous stretch of water in the world because so many pirates operated there.

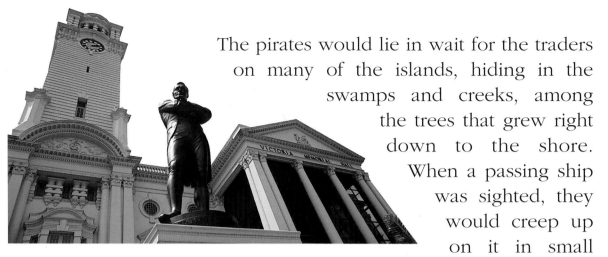

The pirates would lie in wait for the traders on many of the islands, hiding in the swamps and creeks, among the trees that grew right down to the shore. When a passing ship was sighted, they would creep up on it in small boats. These boats were manned by slaves, which left the pirates free to jump aboard and take their European victims by surprise.

In 1819, an Englishman named Stamford Raffles set up a British settlement on Singapore—an island off the southern tip of Malaysia. The land had been bought from a local ruler, the Temenggong of Johore. There were lots of pirates in the region, and one of the worst was the Temenggong himself. Many of the native islanders acted as his spies and would inform him when a merchant ship left the harbor. Afterward, he rewarded his spies by letting them deal in stolen goods.

Above: A statue of Stamford Raffles, who founded a British colony in Singapore and swore to wipe out piracy in the region. He was also a famous naturalist and discovered a rare plant called *Rafflesia*. He was born in 1781 and died in 1826.

Below: Two groups of Dayak pirates, traveling in swift boats called *prahus*, attack Rajah James Brooke's men in 1843. The Englishmen, in a similar craft named the *Jolly Batchelor*, eventually destroyed one *prahu* and killed the crew of the other.

The pirate destroyer

The British explorer and adventurer, James Brooke, who had become the "rajah," or ruler, of a kingdom in Sarawak, decided that trade could only be profitable if piracy were stamped out. Working with naval officer Henry Keppel, he destroyed the bases of Singapore's Sariba pirates, and then did the same to the Dayaks, a group that operated around Borneo. Encouraged by Keppel's success, and by the offer of £20 per pirate killed or captured, other officers joined the fight. In 1849, after destroying 88 Dayak pirate boats, Captain Farquhar of the ship *The Albatross* claimed £20,700—equivalent to 1,035 pirates.

One by one the pirate strongholds were destroyed. But piracy in the East was not wiped out completely. Sea robbers continue to harass traders to this very day. Indeed, the last few years have seen a revival of the pirates' deadly trade.

Sir Henry Keppel, the commander of the *Dido*, helped James Brooke to clear the seas around Borneo of pirate fleets.

The spine-chilling Bugis

One group of pirates and traders whose very name sent chills down a European trader's spine were the Bugis. These expert seamen traveled all the way from New Guinea to Sumatra, and for many years they were the leading traders in the area. They also took slaves and attacked settlements—and they never turned up their noses at a stray British ship. Even the name of these Bugi-men must have been frightening, as it was similar to the word "bogeyman."

TIME LINE

A.D. 1500	1650	1800

2000 B.C.
Phoenicians begin trading throughout Mediterranean

75 B.C.
Julius Caesar captured by pirates

67 B.C.
Pompey defeats Cilician pirates

1492
Christopher Columbus sails to America

1497
Vasco da Gama sails around Cape of Good Hope

1504
Aruj Barbarossa captures two of the Pope's ships

1516
Aruj Barbarossa dies

1523
Start of piracy in Caribbean

1530
Knights of St. John move base to Malta

1543
Spanish treasure ships first sail in fleets

1570
Francis Drake's first privateering voyage

1601
First voyage of British East India Company

1630
Start of buccaneering in Caribbean

1661
Cheng Chih-lung beheaded

1670
Henry Morgan attacks Panama

1695
Henry Avery captures Mogul emperor's ship

1696
Captain Kidd sets out to capture Henry Avery

1701
Kidd hanged for piracy

1713
Treaty of Utrecht. Many sailors turn to piracy

1718
Death of Blackbeard

1720
Mary Read and Anne Bonny captured

1811
Ching Shih surrenders her pirate fleet

1830
Last corsairs in Mediterranean are rounded up

1849
Pirate fleets of Shap-'ng-tsai and Chui Apoo destroyed by British Navy

GLOSSARY

Admiral A naval officer of the highest rank.
Brethren Brothers.
Buccaneer A pirate, usually from a European country, who operated in the Atlantic, Caribbean, and Indian oceans.
Code of conduct An official set of rules.
Coffer A chest in which to keep treasure.
Colonize To settle in and rule over another country.
Corsairs Pirates who operated in the Mediterranean Sea.
Deserter Someone who runs away from service, in the army or navy, for example.
Dey Local leader of a Muslim country.
Empire A group of countries united, usually by force, under the leadership of one country.
Galleon A large ship of the type used by the Spanish in the sixteenth century.
Galley A low, flat-built vessel with sails and oars.

Governor Someone who rules a state or region, or rules a country in place of a king or queen.
Hold A ship's storeroom.
Junk A large, flat-bottomed boat used in Far-Eastern countries, especially China.
Kegs Small barrels.
Knight A member of a military Christian order founded in the Middle Ages to combat Islam.
Letter of marque An official, written permit allowing pirates to plunder enemy ships.
Maroon To leave behind in a deserted place.
Phoenicians A group of famous traders who dominated the Mediterranean in ancient times.
Plantation A large area of land used for growing crops.
Privateers Pirates working with the permission of their governments.
Strait A narrow stretch of water between areas of land.

FURTHER INFORMATION

FURTHER READING

Martell, Hazel Mary. *The Age of Discovery, 1500–1650*. The Illustrated History of the World. New York: Facts on File, 1993.

McWilliams, Karen. *Pirates*. First Books: New York: Franklin Watts, 1989.

Stevenson, Robert Louis. *Treasure Island*. First published 1883. New York: Puffin Books, 1984.

For Older Readers

Defoe, Daniel and Knill, Harry. *Pirates*. Santa Barbara: Bellerophron Books, 1975.

Esquemeling, John. *The Buccaneers of America*. Originally published in 1678. New York: Dorset Press, 1984. Many of the anecdotes in *Pirates and Treasure* come from Esquemeling's classic.

Fraser, George MacDonald. *The Pyrates!* New York: Plume Books, 1985.

Morley, David. *Pirates and Privateers of the Americas: An Illustrated Encyclopedia*. Boulder: ABC-CLIO, 1994.

MOVIES

The Black Swan (1942) Historical adventure that features Captain Henry Morgan.

Captain Blood (1935) Classic black-and-white film starring Errol Flynn.

Captain Kidd (1945) Charles Laughton stars as the infamous privateer.

Shipwrecked (1991) and *Treasure Island* (filmed in 1934, 1950, 1972, and 1990) Both are based on famous adventure novels by Robert Louis Stevenson that feature pirates.

Several of the paintings reproduced in this book are the work of American artist Howard Pyle. Pyle (1853–1911) was a writer and illustrator and illustrated a number of books for young readers, including *The Merry Adventures of Robin Hood* (1883) and *Stolen Treasure* (1907). His work is seen on this book's cover and title page, and on pages 23 (bottom), 24 (top), 27, 36.

INDEX